Voices of
the Australian bush

Harold J. Pollock

THE JACARANDA PRESS

First published 1970 by
THE JACARANDA PRESS
65 Park Road, Milton, Qld
151 Victoria Road, Gladesville, N.S.W.
83 Palmerston Crescent, South Melbourne, Vic.
142 Colin Street, West Perth, W.A.
303 Wright Street, Adelaide, S.A.
4 Kirk Street, Grey Lynn, Auckland 2, N.Z.

Typeset in 9/10 pt Helios Light

Metric edition 1979
Printed in Hong Kong

© Harold J. Pollock 1970, 1979

National Library of Australia
Cataloguing-in-Publication data

Pollock, Harold J.
    Voices of the Australian bush.
    Metricated ed.
    First published, Brisbane: Jacaranda, 1970.
    ISBN 0 7016 1200 2
    1. Animal sounds. I. Title.
591.59'0994

Preface

This book and record, like others I have produced for The Jacaranda Press, are published with the prime idea of interesting people, particularly young people, in identifying some of our 700-odd species of native birds; from their descriptions, their pictures, and, most of all, from their voices.

It is a proven fact that the more people know about our indigenous animals the more likely they are to want to protect them, and, more important, to make sure they are here for future generations to see and hear. In order to make certain that not one species of native animal is lost through the rapid spread of civilization into wilderness areas, it is all important to see that large areas of pristine bushland and other animal habitats are set aside as national parks and reserves, for all time.

At present less than 1.5 per cent of our land is so reserved. A United Nations study recommended that the minimum area any country should set aside for parks and natural reserves should be 5 per cent. It is an indictment on our government that such a tiny portion of this great, wonderful land has so far been reserved for this purpose.

Every living animal, including man, is dependent on its environment for survival. Not one creature could live on this planet without vegetation. If all vegetation were removed, the earth would quickly become a dead planet; as lifeless as the waterless moon. Today, with greatly increased industrialization, transport and such things, the need to conserve our natural environment is greater than ever before.

We ourselves, the other mammals, the birds, reptiles, fishes and different living things are in great danger from pollution of the soil, water and air.

That great conservation body, the National Audubon Society of America, is doing a great deal to encourage preservation of the natural environment. It has succinctly set out the principles of ecology in its *Statement of Audubon Philosophy*. May I quote a few lines from this philosophy:

We believe in the wisdom of nature's design. We know the soil, water, plants and wild creatures depend upon each other and are vital to human life.

We recognize that each living thing links to many others in the chain of nature.

We believe that persistent research into the intricate patterns of outdoor life will help to assure wise use of earth's abundance.

We condemn no wild creature and work to assure that no living species shall be lost.

We believe that every generation should be able to experience spiritual and physical refreshment in places where primitive nature is undisturbed. So we will be vigilant to protect wilderness areas, refuges and parks, and to encourage good use of nature's storehouse of resources.

We dedicate ourselves to the pleasant task of opening the eyes of young and old that all may come to enjoy the beauty of the outdoor world, and to share in conserving its wonders forever.

Harold J. Pollock

Introduction

I suppose mine is a unique job as far as Australia is concerned. For the past twenty years I have travelled thousands of kilometres of outback Australia, listening, observing, photographing, and recording the voices of many native birds, mammals, reptiles and insects. During this time, under the sponsorship of the Bank of New South Wales, I have produced the first life-history films that have been made of the Brolga, the Egrets, the Australian Pelican, the Superb Lyrebird, the flightless birds of New Zealand and Australia, the Koala and now the magnificent Red Kangaroo, the Cassowary and the Emu.

While I was shooting these films I learned a great deal of the fascinating ways of much of our unique fauna. For months at a time, far from the noise and rush of the great cities, I would sit in my little tent-hide, parked perhaps on the shady banks of a great river, or beside a quiet drinking-hole far out in the west. My long-focus lens would record intimate details (which few people have the pleasure of seeing) of the domestic life of shy creatures in their natural environment. My microphone, fixed to a thirty-metre cable, would record their voices, even when these were little more than a whisper.

From my now extensive library of colour pictures and bird-calls I have made a selection of twenty-nine birds; some well-known to any keen bird-watcher, others even some of the experts seldom see or hear. I have tried to make my selection as comprehensive as possible, and for this reason have included one or two representatives from different groups of birds. The raptors are represented by the great Wedge-tailed Eagle and the Whistling Kite. Then come the bower-birds and the catbirds which have various calls of a most unusual nature for feathered animals.

The forest dwellers include one of the world's most accomplished bird-mimics, the Albert Lyrebird, whose photograph is claimed to be the first ever taken of this shy fellow in his natural habitat. The Brown Pigeon, the sweet-voiced Golden Whistler and the Buff-breasted Pitta complete the representatives from the shady, lofty forests.

Australia has two figbirds, the yellow variety of northern Australia being the chosen representative in this book.

The Island Continent was called by early mapmakers the 'Land of Parrots', for we have more varieties of this colourful, noisy throng than any other country, except South America. The Eastern and Crimson Rosellas, two of our most colourful and sweet-voiced parrots, together with the raucous-voiced Sulphur-crested Cockatoo and the wailing Yellow-tailed Black Cockatoo have been chosen.

The quaint, nimble little Willy Wagtail has the honour of opening Side Two of the record. Then follows the Brown Honeyeater whose sweet melody would charm any wayside lingerer.

The cuckoo family is represented by the Pallid Cuckoo, whose call, ascending the scale, is easily recognized during spring and summer throughout much of Australia, and the Coucal or Swamp Pheasant, the only Australian cuckoo that builds its own nest.

Next comes the Rainbow-bird, as colourful as a feathered butterfly, and the 'ya-hooing' Grey-crowned Babbler.

The well-known Spur-winged Plover introduces the swamp and water birds. Then follows that clown on land and master of the air and water, the Australian Pelican, and his noisy offspring.

Next, the handsome Cape Barren Goose and the disappearing Magpie Goose.

One of the best-known of the swamp birds is the White-headed Stilt, which often disturbs the slumber of the air with its dog-like, yapping calls.

Surely the Black Swan has one of the most pleasant and musical voices of all Australian water-birds.

To the tiny Reed Warbler goes the honour of closing this book and record. This superb warbler, so difficult to see and easy to hear, has the distinction of being distantly related to the European Nightingale. In fact, some of its warbling notes are not unlike those of its famous Northern Hemisphere relative.

It is my keenest wish that those who read *Voices of the Australian Bush* and listen to the record will be encouraged to become bird-observers, or bird-watchers — call them what you will.

The years I have spent in the great 'Back of Beyond', observing birds and mammals going about their everyday lives, have been the most rewarding of my life. My health has improved; my eyesight and hearing have taken on a keeness I did not think possible. But, best of all, I have learned to live a relaxed life close to nature, and to achieve a sense of oneness with the universe it would be hard to acquire in any other way.

Young or old, you can easily do likewise. You might even, by reading my book, be tempted to try your hand at recording bird-calls. At the close of the book I gladly give you secrets of recording I have learned over long years of trial and error.

Side 1

1. Wedge-tailed Eagle

(Aquila audax)

Also called Eagle-hawk. It is found over most of Australia and also in Tasmania. Why this magnificent bird should be reduced to the status of a hawk is hard to understand, considering the fact that it is the fourth-largest living eagle.

Easily the largest of the Australian birds-of-prey, the Wedge-tailed Eagle has been ruthlessly hunted and shot, almost since the beginning of white settlement. It has been given a bad reputation as a lamb killer, but from recent research on the species it seems that lamb forms only a very small part of its diet.

Amateur naturalists who have searched Wedge-tailed Eagles' nests also reported that the majority of bones and remains found there are those of rabbits. Wedge-tails also feed on young Dingoes, marsupials and birds. On the whole, evidence seems to indicate that the Wedge-tailed Eagle does a lot more good than harm in its control of undesirable animals.

The great nest is usually built in a high eucalyptus tree so that the sitting bird has a commanding view of the surrounding country. The clutch comprises one or two, and occasionally three, eggs coloured white or light buff. This recording was made from a tame but free bird owned by Mr Eric Ixer, Manager of the Townsville Zoological Gardens, Queensland.

The Wedge-tailed Eagle is now protected throughout Australia.

2. Whistling Kite

(Haliastur sphenurus)

This interesting predator, also known as the Whistling Eagle and Carrion Hawk, is found over most of Australia and very rarely in Tasmania; it also occurs in New Guinea and New Caledonia. To me the ascending trill of the call of the Whistling Eagle is one of the most cheerful sounds to be heard anywhere in the Australian bush. The call is quite loud and can be heard about a kilometre away.

A scavenger near water, it feeds on dead fish and offal. It also eats small mammals, birds, reptiles, carrion and insects. In some districts, as with the Wedge-tailed Eagle, rabbits provide an item of diet. Its prey is nearly always taken from the ground and not caught in the air.

The rather large flat nest is built of sticks lined with leaves, and is placed on a horizontal branch of a tall tree. The clutch comprises two or three eggs, white or bluish-white, sparsely spotted lavender and reddish-brown. The recording was made from a captive bird in Mr David Fleay's sanctuary at Burleigh Heads, southern Queensland.

3. Satin Bower-bird

(Ptilonorhynchus violaceus)

The Satin Bower-bird is also called the Satin-bird. I wonder if nature has ever used more lustrous hues. When viewed in strong sunlight the metallic sheen of the coat of this handsome bird is almost startling in its intensity. The species frequents forest areas along the eastern seaboard from the Atherton Tablelands, Queensland, to the Otway Ranges, Victoria. Food comprises wild fruits, berries and insects.

The bower, usually built under an overhanging tree or shrub, is about forty centimetres long and thirty-five centimetres high. It is built on thin sticks placed upright into a platform of the same materials. Objects used in decorating the bower are nearly always blue, yellowish-green or creamy-yellow. Decorations include such objects as bluebags, blue matchboxes, blue cigarette packets, blue feathers, blue pegs, blue glass, blue marbles, sweet papers, snail shells, cicada cases and yellowish-green leaves.

The typical churring call of the Satin Bower-bird is to me one of the most exciting sounds to be heard in nature. I never fail to get a thrill when walking in the bush I hear this call coming from some shrub or thicket in the near vicinity. A young lad, who was watching a Satin Bower-bird playing in its museum, when he heard the churring call exclaimed, 'Listen, he's winding up his clock!'

The nest is usually built of thin twigs of the same thickness and composition as those of which the bower is built. The clutch comprises two or three eggs, dark green, spotted brown and slate-grey. Mr Norman Robinson of Western Australia made this excellent record at Tidbinbilla, Australian Capital Territory. Notice that at the end of the recording the bird mimics a Laughing Kookaburra and a Raven, whilst singing his own song at the same time. Mr Robinson says that, in his experience, adult male Satin Bower-birds often end their songs with mimicry of this kind.

4. Great Bower-bird

(Chlamydera nuchalis)

The Great Bower-bird is the largest of the seven species of bower-birds found in Australia. Distribution is from the Kimberleys through tropical northern Australia to a little south of Mackay, Queensland. The bowers are mostly built under a thorny thicket; they are usually about sixty centimetres in length, forty-five centimetres wide and about forty centimetres high, with the walls curving in at the top. The inside of the bower roughly fits the curve of the bird's body. Decorations are generally made up of land-snail shells, bits of bleached coral, bleached bones, flowers and green fruit. When the bower is built near civilization, man-made objects often make their appearance in the bird's museum. Clothes pegs, pens, pencils, children's toys, pieces of glass, coins and even a glass eye have been found in different bowers.

Like its satin-blue relation, the Great Bower-bird has a keen sense of colour. I have seen it remove immature oranges from the bower as soon as they became yellow. It then replaced the tiny, yellow oranges with fresh green ones. I once placed all the yellowed oranges back in the bower. When the owner returned, with much scolding he promptly removed the yellow oranges and threw them in all directions. Many people confuse the bower with the nest, which is always built in a tree, sometimes as high as twenty metres above the ground. The nest is open and composed of twigs of the same texture and composition as those of the bower. The clutch comprises one or two beautifully marked and coloured eggs. Food comprises seeds, fruits, berries and insects.

When the Great Bower-bird makes the 'chip chip chipping' call you hear in the record, he usually does a neat little song-and-dance number in, out and around his bower. At such times he gets himself low to the ground, spreads his wings, raises the purple crest on the nape of the neck and does his stiff-legged, hopping dance, which is most engaging to watch.

I made this record with the microphone placed about sixty centimetres from a bower made in a backyard garden in Townsville, North Queensland.

SIDE 1

△
1. Wedge-tailed Eagle

△
2. Whistling Kite. Also known as the Whistling Eagle.
Ellis McNamara

◁
3. Satin Bower-bird
Recorded by *Norman Robinson*

4. Great Bower-bird
▽

5. Green Catbird. *Norman Chaffer*

6. Spotted Catbird. *Jack Purnell*

8. Brown Pigeon. *Ellis McNamara*

7. Albert Lyrebird. *H.S. Curtis*, national parks biologist, Queensland Department of Forestry

5. Green Catbird

(Ailuroedus crassirostris)

Related to the bower-birds are the two species of catbirds found in Australia. Their voices are among the most unusual of any birds. One of their calls greatly resembles the miaowing of an alley tomcat on the prowl. In some parts of Queensland the Green Catbird is often referred to as the 'Crybaby Bird.' One Queensland naturalist always avers that the call of the Green Catbird sounds like 'Here I arrrrrre.'

Distribution is from south-eastern Queensland and eastern New South Wales south to the vicinity of the Clyde River. I first heard the Green Catbird and made this recording in the magnificent rain-forest at Cunningham's Gap, southern Queensland. It was just on nightfall and it was certainly a weird experience to hear the yowling calls coming from the depths of the rain-forest. The Green Catbird builds a bowl-shaped nest which is sometimes lined with moss and fine twigs. The usual clutch is two eggs, cream or pale creamy-white.

6. Spotted Catbird

(Ailuroedus melanotis)

This Catbird is found in northern Queensland from Cape York to Cardwell. It is also native to the Aru Islands and southern New Guinea. Habits, diet and calls are very similar to those of its close relative. This recording of the Spotted Catbird was made on a sunny morning in the rain-forest growing on the banks of Lake Barrine, Atherton Tablelands. To hear the dawn chorus in that picturesque area is a memorable experience. The Spotted Catbird's miaowing calls always form a prominent part of it. Nest and eggs are very similar to those of the Green Catbird.

7. Albert Lyrebird

(Menura alberti)

The Albert Lyrebird has the reputation of being just as accomplished at mimicry as its better-known relative, the Superb Lyrebird, although I have never had evidence of this. Nevertheless it is a remarkable mimic of other birds' calls and bush sounds. It is found from the Richmond River (north-eastern New South Wales) in rain-forest country, to south-eastern Queensland.

The Albert species is smaller and more rufous in plumage than the Superb variety. It also differs in that, as far as is known, it never builds mounds, but displays in favoured clearings, on low branches and on fallen logs. Its territorial call differs from that of its southern relative, having an echoing, ringing quality that is impossible to describe.

The nest, a bulky structure with a side-entrance, is built of sticks, dried fern-leaves and the like, and is lined with downy feathers from the female's flanks. It breeds in the winter months, laying a single egg which takes six weeks to incubate. The young bird is fed in the nest for another six weeks. In the coldest months of winter, in the McPherson Ranges, I stalked the male bird for days on end, hoping to take a passable photo of the shy fellow, but never once was I successful. I came to the conclusion that the Albert Lyrebird can hear one breathe, so difficult is it to approach. My congratulations to Sydney Curtis who succeeded where I failed; also my thanks to him for allowing me to publish for the first time a photo of a wild Albert Lyrebird.

I made the recording in the rain-forest at Mount Tamborine, south-eastern Queensland, early one winter's morning. After a painful scramble through clinging vines and undergrowth, I managed to get behind a log about ten metres from a calling bird. The microphone was set on focus within the parabolic reflector. The very first item is *alberti's* territorial call.

8. Brown Pigeon

(Macropygia amboinensis)

Distribution of the Brown Pigeon is from the Northern Territory and eastern Queensland to south-eastern New South Wales. It is also native to the Philippine Islands and New Guinea. Its other names include Brownie, Pheasant Pigeon and Large-tailed Pigeon.

It feeds mainly on the berries of the ink-weed and those of wild tobacco and wild raspberry. This bird of the big forests prefers the margins of bush tracks and more open parts. Its monotonous 'whoop-a-whoop' calls form a leading part of the dawn chorus of the rain-forests of Queensland.

The nest is a flimsy platform of sticks, laid crosswise in a tangle of vines or sometimes on the horizontal branches of a rain-forest tree. The bird lays a single creamy-white egg, usually from October to December; but the breeding season varies a good deal according to locality.

9. Golden Whistler

(Pachycephala pectoralis)

Distribution is eastern and southern Australia, from Cairns to Eyre Peninsula; the bird is also found in south-western Australia and Tasmania. It is sometimes known as the Yellow-breasted Whistler, White-throated Whistler or Thunderbird. This is one of the most common birds to be heard, and is occasionally seen in the magnificent rain-forests of southern Queensland. It has been termed 'Thunderbird' because of its strange habit of calling immediately after it hears thunder or any other loud noise.

If we rated our Australian birds according to their singing ability, I would give the Golden Whistler a very high placing. As you hear from the record, this beautiful songster has a range of calls of great variety and tonal quality. An insect-eater, it builds a cup-shaped shallow nest made of rootlets and plant stems. The clutch comprises two or three stone-coloured or white speckled brown eggs. This recording was made at dawn in the lush rain-forest on Mount Tamborine, Queensland. I used a parabolic reflector to amplify the call and to cut out extraneous noises coming from the rear of the rubber-coated reflector.

10. Buff-breasted Pitta

(Pitta versicolor)

The specific name of this colourful bird, *versicolor*, is certainly well chosen. It is also called the Noisy Pitta, Dragoon-bird, Painted Thrush, Anvil-bird, and Bob-tail. Essentially a bird of the 'big scrub', as the rain-forest or jungle country is popularly known in Australia, the Buff-breasted Pitta also has a distinctive call which cannot be confused with that of any other bird. Its chief call has often been said to resemble the words 'walk-to-work' or 'want-a-watch'. Like the Pallid Cuckoo, it is very susceptible to the sound of its own voice being replayed on a tape recorder; in fact it can often be called quite close by just giving a rough imitation of its 'walk-to-work' call. In the rain-forests of tropical Queensland the Buff-breasted Pitta always takes a notable place in the orchestra that supplies the music of the morning chorus. It is found over most of eastern Australia from Cape York to coastal central New South Wales.

Almost entirely a ground-dweller, it feeds on land-snails and insects. It is adept at breaking the shells of land-snails; for this purpose it bashes the shell on a stone, which is often referred to as its 'anvil'. The surrounds of the anvils soon become littered with empty snail-shells.

Three or four, sometimes five, creamy-white eggs splotched with blackish-brown form the clutch.

The recording was made in the rain-forest on Tamborine Mountain one early spring morning.

9. Golden Whistler. *Ellis McNamara*

10. Buff-breasted Pitta. Also known as the Noisy Pitta. *Ellis McNamara*

11. Yellow Figbird. *Norman Chaffer*

12. Eastern Rosella. *Ellis McNamara*

△ 13. Crimson Rosella

△ 15. Sulphur-crested Cockatoo

△ 14. Yellow-tailed Black Cockatoo. *Donald Tronnson and Molly Clampett*

▷

Harold J. Pollock recording bird calls with his parabolic reflector and Uher Recorder. Taken at Jerilderie, western New South Wales

11. Yellow Figbird

(Sphecotheres flaviventris)

This interesting bird is found in the Northern Territory and north-eastern Queensland. It likes different types of forest and is not averse to visiting the orchards or garden fruit-trees in its locality.

The slow, measured beat of the Yellow Figbird's repeated call is one of the most attractive sounds heard in northern Queensland. Its food comprises native fruits and berries. The nest is saucer-shaped and the three eggs are greenish, spotted with reddish-brown or purplish-red.

12. Eastern Rosella

(Platycercus eximius)

The Eastern Rosella is found from southern Queensland to Victoria, and in south-eastern South Australia and Tasmania. It feeds mainly on grass-seeds, wild fruits and berries.

Most members of the great Australian parrot group have harsh voices, but the Eastern Rosella is certainly a pleasant exception to this rule. The cheery whistling notes of this handsome bird are some of the most musical sounds to be heard in the Australian bush. Like some others of the parrot family, it breeds in a hole in a tree-stump, or sometimes in a fence-post. The clutch comprises four to nine white eggs and the breeding season is during spring and summer.

13. Crimson Rosella

(Platycercus elegans)

This magnificent bird has local names such as Crimson Parrot, Red Lowry and Mountain Lowry. The Crimson Rosella is one of the most colourful of all the Australian parrots. It has a wide distribution from Queensland to Victoria, South Australia, Kangaroo and King Islands and Norfolk Island.

A seed-eater, the bird is also fond of blossoms, fruit and berries. It sometimes takes fruit from orchards, but offsets this offence because it eats quantities of scale-insects. Like the Eastern Rosella, it has many musical notes, some of which are borrowed by that master-mocker, the Superb Lyrebird. This bird photographs remarkably well on colour film. During a recent lecture-tour for the National Audubon Society of America, I featured the Crimson Rosella in my lecture film; almost every time the beautiful bird flashed on the screen there was an audible gasp of admiration from the audience. Like most members of the parrot family, the Crimson Rosella nests in a hole in a tree and lays from five to eight white eggs.

This recording was made near O'Reilly's Guest House in the McPherson Ranges, Queensland: a magnificent locality for anyone interested in watching or listening to native birds.

14. Yellow-tailed Black Cockatoo

(Calyptorhynchus funereus)

A handsome black parrot, sometimes called the Funereal Cockatoo. It feeds mostly on seeds of such trees and shrubs as banksias, casuarinas and hakeas, and tears the bark and wood of eucalypts with its powerful bill in order to uncover large white grubs. The flight is rather laboured and slow. When flying it often utters loud wailing cries of 'Kee-ah, kee-ah'. This elegant black bird has acquired quite a reputation as a rain prophet. Some country people say that if black cockatoos appear in unaccustomed places, rain will fall within a short time.

The clutch usually comprises three or four white eggs which are laid in a nest in a hole in a tree. The recording was made on Tamborine Mountain, Queensland.

15. Sulphur-crested Cockatoo

(Cocatua galerita)

This beautiful white bird is famous the world over as a cage-bird. It usually feeds on seeds and roots, but sometimes damages crops. When flying against the light in a large flock these birds present a beautiful picture in white and yellow.

The species is found over much of Australia, including Tasmania; also in New Guinea and New Britain. It usually lays two white eggs in a hole in a tree or a cliff face.

SIDE 2

1. Willy Wagtail. *Norman Chaffer*

3. Pallid Cuckoo. *Ellis McNamara*

2. Brown Honeyeater. *Norman Chaffer*

4. Coucal or Swamp Pheasant

△ 5. Rainbow-bird. *Norman Chaffer*

△ 6. Grey-crowned Babbler. *Norman Chaffer*

△ 7. Spur-winged Plover

▷ 8. Australian Pelican

Side 2

1. Willy Wagtail

(Rhipidura leucophrys)

The perky little Willy Wagtail, or Black and White Fly-catcher, is one of the most popular birds in Australia, particularly with country school children. It is likely to be found everywhere from city parks and backyard gardens to the great stations of the outback. I have even seen Willy Wagtails hunting for insects on the lush lawns of Mary Kathleen uranium mine, in north-western Queensland.

Like the rest of the many black and white birds found in Australia, Willy Wagtail is not lacking in courage. In the nesting season it will attack much larger birds such as owls, kookaburras, crows, ravens and butcher-birds. These predators patiently wait an opportunity to steal the chicks when the wagtails relax their guard for a moment. Although the smaller birds usually lose all their young on such occasions, for days they vigorously defend their nest, even if only one chick remains.

The neat cup-shaped nest is built of fine grasses woven together by spider-webbing. The usual clutch comprises three or four eggs which are greyish in colour, and spotted with brown markings on the larger end. In a good season a pair of Willy Wagtails will sometimes raise three broods. This recording was made on the showground at Ulmarra, just north of Grafton in New South Wales. I had my caravan parked under shady trees in the showground-cum-caravan-park where a pair of wagtails were calling in the branches above. I pushed the microphone up through the hatch of the caravan and thus succeeded in obtaining the recording.

Spur-winged Plovers and Magpies can be heard calling in the background.

2. Brown Honeyeater

(Lichmera indistincta)

The loud and animated calls of the Brown Honeyeater are among the most distinctive made by any Australian song-bird; perhaps the strongest of any small Australian bird. The calls are not unlike those of the Reed Warbler. These lively brown birds inhabit the coastal mangroves and shrublands; also the scrubs of the sub-interior. Their food is insects and nectar.

The suspended, small, cup-shaped nest is composed of soft bark and fibre lined with plant-down. It is often built near water. The usual clutch comprises two eggs, white with a few specks of pale chestnut on the larger end.

This recording was obtained just north of Marlborough, central Queensland. Before I took an afternoon nap on a sunny spring day, I placed my microphone on the edge of a little stream which was running through lush vegetation. With a lead of 50 metres of shielded cable attached to the microphone and my recorder, I waited until the honeyeaters commenced their melodious chorus and thus made the record.

3. Pallid Cuckoo

(Cuculus pallidus)

The Pallid Cuckoo, also called Semitone-bird and Scale-bird, has one of the most distinctive calls of all Australian birds. It occasionally varies the typical ascending call with both harsh and musical notes. Bird recordists and photographers, myself included, often play back the call of a bird to get it to approach closer so that a better photograph or recording may be obtained. Some species respond to this technique much more readily than others. The Pallid Cuckoo 'falls' for this neat trick every time. Recently I was camped on a sheep station at Coree, near Jerilderie, western New South Wales, when I called up a Pallid Cuckoo with my recorder. So successful was the ruse that I obtained excellent photographs and recordings; but then I could not get rid of the bird, which persisted throughout the day, calling close to where I was camped. This time I understood why the Pallid Cuckoo was sometimes termed Brain-fever Bird.

It is a migrant to south-eastern Australia, arriving in July or August and usually departing in February or March, although a few birds may remain throughout the year. This cuckoo is a useful ally of man because its chief item of diet is caterpillars, especially those with hairlike bristles which few other birds will take. Like most other cuckoos, it is parasitic and more than eighty species have been recorded as foster-parents to Pallid Cuckoo chicks. The egg is of a uniform flesh colour, sometimes with a few dots of a darker hue.

The recording was made at Lone Pine Sanctuary, near Brisbane. I had my caravan parked under a spreading eucalypt and the previous evening I had attached a microphone to a branch of the tree, hoping that I might pick up a few bird-calls in the morning. The Pallid Cuckoo came and perched quite close to the microphone, which enabled me to get this excellent recording.

4. Coucal or Swamp Pheasant

(Centropus phasianinus)

This brown bird of the creeks, swamps and regions of rank blade and other grasses has a wide range of habitats from north-west to western Australia, through northern and eastern Australia south to the Nowra district of New South Wales. Most Australians call this bird the Swamp Pheasant; a misnomer because it does not belong to the pheasant family but is correctly grouped with the cuckoos.

It is a fairly common bird and its call, which has been described as sounding like 'coop, coop, coop', or 'book, book, book', repeated a number of times, cannot be confused with the call of any other Australian species. It is much easier to identify the Coucal from its call than by sighting it, although it is sometimes seen sitting in low shrubs or flying in clumsy fashion across a roadway. Its food comprises frogs, small reptiles, aquatic insects, and the eggs and young of other birds. The Coucal has the distinction of being the only Australian member of the cuckoo family that builds its own nest and raises its own chicks. The nest, a football-shaped structure, is constructed of grass and sticks and is open at both ends. It is usually built in a tussock of tall grass formed by joining the tops of the grasses together and lining the inside with leaves; occasionally nests are found in low shrubs. The eggs are chalky white.

The recording was made on a farm in the Rockhampton district, central Queensland. I had parked my caravan for the night near a spreading bush. Just before sundown I heard a Coucal call in this bush. I placed my microphone under the bush and attached it to a lead, the other end of which I had in the caravan. In the morning the Coucal obliged with the hearty performance you hear on this record.

5. Rainbow-bird

(Merops ornatus)

The Rainbow-bird, or Bee-eater, is another brilliantly coloured Australian species. It is Australia's one representative of more than twenty kinds of these birds which are found in many parts of the tropical and temperate zone of the old world. It is quite easy

19

△ 9. Pelican chicks in the nest

△ 10. Pelican chick just able to walk

 11. Cape Barren Goose

△ 12. Pied Goose or Magpie Goose

△ 13. Pied Stilt. *Ellis McNamara*

△ 14. Black Swan and chicks

△ 15. Reed Warbler. *Ellis McNamara*

to distinguish the Rainbow-bird from other Australian species because of its size (about that of a starling, though slimmer), its colourful plumage, and the fact that it has two spine-like feathers projecting from the end of the tail. In the southern part of Australia it is a migrant, usually arriving in October and leaving late in January or during February and March. Many of the birds migrate to the islands north of Australia. In northern parts many of the birds remain throughout the year.

Graceful but erratic in flight, the Rainbow-bird captures insects, its main item of food, on the wing. It has often raised the ire of bee-keepers because it feeds on both native and domestic bees. But, like many of our native birds, it probably does more good than harm in the fact that it captures harmful insects such as dragon-flies and robber-flies which are both known predators of bees. It also eats large numbers of other insects and will even fly into water to capture food. The calls of the Rainbow-bird are shrill, animated and often given on the wing. These notes can not easily be confused with those of any other Australian bird.

The nesting habits of the species are interesting in that it digs a sloping tunnel up to about one metre long into sandy or loamy soil. A cavity is made at the end of the tunnel to contain the eggs. Five to seven white glossy eggs usually form the clutch.

This recording was made at Yarrawonga, Victoria, during early summer. I found a pair with a nesting tunnel. When they returned from foraging trips with food for the young they invariably alighted on a branch nearby, before flying to the burrow-entrance with the food. I tied the microphone close to this landing perch and thus obtained the recording.

6. Grey-crowned Babbler

(Pomatostomus temporalis)

In different localities the Grey-crowned Babbler is also known as the Apostle-bird, Cackler, Catbird, Codlin-moth-eater, Arco and Happy Family. This interesting bird of the scrubs and open forests, usually some distance from the coast, has one of the most cheery calls of all our native birds. Its main call note is a clamant 'yaa-hoo, yaa-hoo, yaa-hoo'. It also has several other chattering, cackling notes. Highly gregarious, it is usually seen in flocks of about eight to twelve; hence the names Twelve Apostles and Happy Family. They spend much time on the ground actively searching for insects, at the same time uttering their quaint chattering or cackling notes.

The nest is a large dome-shaped affair with a hood over the entrance. It is built of loosely interwoven twigs and sticks and lined with bark fibre, feathers, grasses and sometimes wool. The species also builds what are known as 'roost nests', which are really communal nests in which babblers crowd at dusk. Three to six buff to purplish-brown eggs are usually laid; they are over-marked with hairlike markings of dark brown.

The recording was made in early spring, at Gillett's Ridge, near Grafton. I was camped there filming the life history of the four species of egrets found in Australia, and would often hear the 'yah-hooing' of the babblers. After many attempts, I finally succeeded in getting near enough to a calling babbler with my microphone set in the parabolic reflector and thus obtained this recording.

7. Spur-winged Plover

(Lobibyx novaehollandiae)

This is a common bird in eastern and southern Australia, including Tasmania, found mainly in swamps, grassy flats and parklands. The distinctive calls are usually given while the birds are in flight. The shrill alarm note warns its companions, as well as other species in the neighbourhood, of possible danger. Food comprises insects, small crustaceans and herbage. The nest is merely a depression in the ground lined with short dried grass-stems. The usual clutch is four greenish-olive eggs which are covered with dark brown spots and markings. Both sexes take turns at incubating the eggs.

It was rather fun securing this record. I set up my small tent-hide about ten metres from a nest I had found at Ulmarra, near Grafton, New South Wales. Placing the microphone on a long lead quite close to the nest, I sat in the hide awaiting the plovers' return, hoping that they would call. Several times they returned, but not once did they call. Then an obliging cow came on the scene and helped considerably. The cow walked near the nest and the two plovers became very agitated and made threats at the cow, at the same time calling loudly.

8. Australian Pelican

(Pelecanus conspicillatus)

On this record you have listened to some of the most melodious bird-calls to be heard in the great Australian outback. Now we come to some of the water-birds, whose voices, generally, although they would not win prizes in an eisteddfod, are still interesting. One of these is the Australian Pelican. It is a strong silent bird, except on occasions when a team is formed to hunt fish; they then utter a few grunting calls. It is found almost throughout Australia, on the islands to the north of the continent and in suitable habitats far into the inland. Apparently, in the early days of settlement, it was something of a mystery as to where the pelican nested. A romantic poem was written at this time bearing the title 'Where the Pelican Builds Her Nest'. Even today, few people have ever seen a pelican's nest. This is because the wary birds nest in colonies on certain islands off the coast, and also on islands in inland lakes. It has been said that if the water dries up, the nesting pelicans will immediately desert the nests, even if the young have hatched.

Food mainly consists of fish although considerable numbers of crustaceans, in both fresh and salt water, are eaten. One, two, or sometimes three, dull white or yellowish-white eggs form the clutch. It has often been assumed that the great bill-pouch is a sort of storehouse for holding fish, but in fact it is used as a scoop for catching fish. Of course, as the bird scoops up the fish in its pouch, it gathers a considerable quantity of water, but this is drained away before the catch is swallowed. It is estimated that the pouch is capable of holding about ten litres of water.

9. Pelican chicks in the nest

The yapping calls of two nestling pelicans have been included because they are most unusual calls for young chicks. The newly-hatched chicks are of a delicate pink shade, almost entirely devoid of feathers. They always remind me of little reptiles of a prehistoric era.

The bill-pouch at this stage is not well developed; it consists merely of a small bag of loose skin which hangs from the lower mandible and the throat.

10. Pelican chick that has just started to walk

The growling, scolding calls of a young pelican just out of the nest are quite distinctive. Its gait can hardly be called a walk, because the young bird is not strong enough to lift its body entirely free of the ground. The abdomen drags along the ground as the bird wobbles awkwardly from side to side, at the same time waving its developing wings to aid locomotion. This and the following recording were obtained from a nesting colony on an island in Lake Alexandrina, South Australia.

11. Cape Barren Goose

(Cereopsis novaehollandiae)

The Cape Barren Goose is also sometimes called Pig Goose, because some of its calls sound very like the grunting of a pig. This handsome bird, with its yellow-and-black beak, brown eyes, grey feathers, pink legs and black feet, is found only in coastal southern Australia and the islands off-shore. A curious fact is that although it is web-footed it is not often seen in the water.

Because it is 'a good table bird', large numbers were formerly shot for the pot. In recent years its numbers have been greatly reduced and it is one of several Australian species that need to be carefully safeguarded. The nest, built of dried grass and plants and lined with down, is large and rather flat. It is always placed on the ground. The clutch comprises four to seven creamy-white eggs.

12. Pied or Magpie Goose

(Anseranas semipalmata)

The bugle-like calls of the Magpie Goose may be heard from a considerable distance. It has a windpipe that may be over one metre long, and which is curled like a French horn. It is also an unusual member of the goose family in that its feet are only partly webbed, or semipalmated. Although formerly it had a much wider distribution, it is now confined mainly to swampy lands in northern Australia and northern New South Wales. It can still be seen in great numbers at Humpty Doo near Darwin. Another interesting place where one can usually see this bird in large numbers is Mount St John Lagoon, at the Townsville Zoological Gardens, where I made this recording.

The nest, built of rushes and herbage, is usually located on a trampled-down tussock of reeds near the centre of a swamp. The clutch comprises about five to eight yellowish-white eggs.

13. Pied Stilt

(Himantopus himantopus)

This elegant, long-legged bird is found almost throughout Australia, wherever suitable habitats occur. It also appears in Tasmania and New Zealand. Its call sounds much like the 'yep, yep, yep' of a puppy. If one inadvertently ventures too near the nest, the nesting birds become greatly agitated, 'yepping' vociferously. I made this recording on a swampy lagoon near Windsor, New South Wales. While the parabolic reflector was held with the microphone set on focus in the air, a pair of birds persistently dive-bombed me, at the same time 'yep, yep, yepping' like angry puppies.

The food consists of insects, snails and other small aquatic animals. Stilts nest in colonies and their nests are quite well constructed of green herbage, grass, rootlets and the like. They are usually built up from the bottom of a shallow lagoon, but at other times the nest is simply a shallow depression in mud, at the margin of a lagoon. The clutch generally comprises four eggs which are greenish-stone in colour, spotted and blotched with greyish-black.

14. Black Swan

(Cygnus atratus)

The honking calls of the Black Swan may be given while the birds are flying in formation overhead, while they are swimming, or even while they are walking on land. The Black Swan's call is quite penetrating and can be heard from some distance. To me it is a very pleasant sound of the swamps and lagoons of outback Australia. An early Dutch explorer, Willem de Vlamingh, found a flock of Black Swans on what is now known as the Swan River, Western Australia. He was so impressed by the unusual colouring of the birds that he captured some of them alive and took them to Batavia. It seems fitting, therefore, that the emblem of Western Australia should be the graceful Black Swan.

During the moulting season these birds are without their primary feathers and so cannot fly. At this time they remain in flocks in secluded waters where their main defence becomes their ability to swim quite swiftly from danger. The nest is a substantial one composed of sticks, rushes, leaves and aquatic plants. It is usually located on an island in a swamp or lake or lagoon. The clutch generally consists of five or six eggs, pale green or dull greenish-white. Both male and female take turns in brooding. Incubation occupies about thirty-five days. The chicks when hatched are little grey balls of fluff. Soon they take to the water and swim well even at this stage. Their enemies are many but the parents fiercely defend the young against any intruder. Their main means of defence are the wings, which are used with such effect that they have been known to break a man's leg.

This recording was made on a farm at Yeppoon, central Queensland. A small flock of wild Black Swans used to come every day to feed with the barnyard fowls. While they were resting in the noonday sun I approached them with my recording gear and obtained the recording.

margin of a lake or lagoon. It is found throughout Australia and Tasmania, wherever a suitable habitat of swamps and reeds is available. It is also frequently heard calling from the reeds on the margins of ornamental lakes of parks and sanctuaries. This sprightly bird is one of our most delightful songsters and is distantly related to the famous Nightingale. For such a small bird the voice is quite far-carrying. It is a migrant to southern Australia, arriving usually during August or September, and departing in March or April. Some birds, however, may remain in the south throughout the winter. The food is insects.

The cup-shaped, elongated nest is made of long soft stems of aquatic plants woven together with debris and lined with softer plant material. It is firmly woven to the stems of the reeds between which it is placed. The eggs, which number three or four, are greyish or bluish-white, faintly spotted with brown or grey. The nesting season is usually from September to December. Notice that the Reed Warbler's calls somewhat resemble those of the Brown Honeyeater. I obtained this recording by placing the microphone in a bed of reeds at the edge of a lagoon at Goolwa, South Australia.

15. Reed Warbler

(Acrocephalus stentoreus)

I have placed the little brown Reed Warbler with the swamp birds because it is so often found in their company, nearly always in reeds growing on the

How I record bird and mammal calls

Let me say at the outset that recording bird and mammal calls is one of the most exciting, frustrating, time-consuming and stimulating of pastimes. Shooting an animal with a camera, or recording its call on tape, is at once a far more difficult and rewarding achievement than blowing the creature to pieces with a gun. In order to achieve success you have to get much closer with the camera or microphone than you do with any firearm.

If you want to make top-quality tape-recordings of animals' calls, you must have a good, reliable portable recorder, if possible of professional standard. It must be battery-operated, run at a constant, accurate rate, and have a speed, if possible, of at least 190 mm per second. In principle, the faster the speed used, the higher the quality of your recordings. Cassette recorders will give quite good quality animal recordings, although not quite the quality of reel-to-reel recorders running at 380 mm per second.

I do not recommend four-track machines, because you cannot play four-track tapes on most professional recorders used in sound studios. A full-track recorder is the ultimate, but a two-track one is still reasonable. I use a two-track version, but make it a practice never to record on the second track. Using the machine in this fashion is certainly not so economical as far as tape is concerned, but it gives the advantage of being able to edit the tapes easily. Also, the tapes can be played direct on to professional studio machines. In other words, by operating in this manner, I gain most of the advantages of owning a full-track recorder.

Make sure the recorder you purchase is a lightweight one. Mine weighs only about 3 kg, complete with battery. You will find I am right in this matter of lightness when you start to hump your cameras and recorder over long distances of unmade tracks in tangled scrub.

What does a recorder such as I have described cost? As in purchasing most kinds of sensitive, finely adjusted instruments, you usually get what you pay for. All I can say is don't, under any circumstances, purchase a cheap recorder for this type of work. If you do, you will be disappointed with the results.

In the top price-bracket is the Swiss Nagra recorder, a precision instrument which is quite expensive. For several years now I have used the German, Uher 4000 Report recorders. These recorders are less expensive but still not cheap. In my opinion this little lightweight machine is a masterpiece of electronic engineering. An extra, which I use, is a rechargeable battery. But the 4000 L will also run on five ordinary torch batteries. The storage battery can be recharged from the cigarette-lighter of a car. All the calls given on this record were made on my trusty little Uher.

A good microphone is a must. The Uher people manufacture several suitable for bird-recording, but there are dozens of other makes on the market. Nearly all microphones are designed to be used only an arm's length or so away from the sound source. So now my greatest recording secret is freely given: 'Get the mike up to the bird.'

This is not always easy, but many times it is quite possible to plant the microphone not more than a metre from a bird's favourite singing perch, or, as with the lyrebird, on a favoured singing mound. Most of the calls given in this record were made with the microphone very close to the singing bird. This desirable result is achieved by previously plotting the bird's favourite singing perch. I often do this on the night previous to recording.

The microphone is connected to a long lead and planted about a metre from the selected perch. At dawn, when most birds sing at their best, I am out and about. The free end of the mike cable is attached to my recorder and I make myself comfortable for a wait of perhaps a few hours. In the end I am usually rewarded with a first-class tape of the bird or mammal I am working with.

If I cannot get the mike up to the bird in the manner described above, I sometimes get good results by aiming my parabolic reflector at a subject I wish to record. The mike is of course set on the focus point and directed in towards the centre of the reflector. The reflector considerably amplifies the recorded sound. But I never use the reflector if it is at all possible to use the extended cable method. Gun microphones are also excellent for bird recording but are very expensive.

When attempting to record a partially shy bird, don't chase it with your equipment. If you do, the bird will probably fly away from you as far as it can. Often I manage to scramble a recording of sorts of a bird I particularly want to tape. I have two machines. On one I play back the indifferent call I have made in an endeavour to entice the bird closer. Very often this ruse succeeds — the bird comes very close and orders my recorder out of its territory by singing at it. Then I bring my second recorder into action and often, in this way, obtain an excellent rendition of its voice. But please don't overdo this technique. Once I had a White-throated Warbler almost frantic by replaying its call close to its nest. The pretty little bird sang and sang at the offending recorder and hovered so close to it that I thought he must eventually disappear inside the instrument. In the end I stopped the playback machine because I was afraid the warbler might become mentally disturbed.

When you have successfully made a fine recording, make an announcement as to the locality, the time of day, the date, the distance the bird was from the mike, weather conditions, and, most important, the name of the bird. If you cannot identify it, then give as full a description as possible; size, colour, markings, colour of legs and bill, length of tail, and any other details which might enable an expert to identify the bird when you ask him. Most experts are very willing to do this, for they, too, are keenly interested in the range and songs of birds. Perhaps you have recorded a species that has never been noted in a particular locality before. Then you may give yourself a pat on the back.

Kia ora (good luck) and good recording

Index